YOUR MARRIAGE

AN OWNER'S MANUAL

BY MARTIN BAXENDALE

ISBN 0 9522032 4 3

Printed in Britain by Stoate & Bishop Printers
Ltd, Cheltenham, Glos

CONTENTS

INTRODUCTION

With care and regular servicing your new Marriage should <u>last a lifetime</u>* and this comprehensive owner's manual is designed to ensure that you enjoy many years of trouble-free and smooth-running wedded bliss.

Carefully following recommended maintenance and servicing procedures will greatly reduce daily wear and tear, minimizing the risk of serious breakdowns and costly repairs, and extending the useful road-life of your Marriage. In particular, it should ease the strain on major components (husband/wife) which is a common cause of irreparable breakdown. Most servicing and maintenance tasks may easily be performed in the home or at a DIY service-station/hotel without the aid of specialist tools or kinky equipment.

* Note: This lifetime guarantee of marital bliss applies <u>only</u> to owners of model XR3i 'Happily-Married'. And even then, it in no way affects your statutory right to whinge, whine, grumble, nag, sulk, squabble, find fault, fall out, pick fights and scream 'Oh God, I want out!' from time to time.

DELIVERY NOTE: We apologise for any delay in the arrival of your long-awaited Marriage but regret that we can accept no liability for circumstances beyond our control; including repeated refusals, rejections or false starts due to lack of commitment or such personal problem factors as chronic spottiness, pongy feet, dandruff, shyness or anti-social personal habits of an unmentionable nature.

MANUFACTURING NOTE: We further regret that most Marriages are <u>not</u>, as frequently advertised, made in Heaven, but are the product of various countries, backgrounds, circumstances, personal relationships and throws of the dice.*

Unfortunately the standard of manufacturing and reliability may not match up to the impossible ideals and over-romanticised dreams you might have been led to expect. A great deal of time-consuming maintenance, servicing and DIY repairs may therefore prove necessary to keep your new Marriage on the road and prevent it falling apart when it hits its first bump or pot-hole. Sorry.

*Note: Your Marriage is also the product of more than one person. Try not to forget it.

PLACES TO GO IN YOUR NEW MARRIAGE:
Once you have mastered the basic controls of your Marriage (see following section) these are just some of the many different and exciting directions you can go in it: Happy-Ever-After Land, To Hell And Back, The Divorce Courts. We strongly advise you to practice your map-reading before setting out.

5

BASIC FEATURES AND CONTROLS

The basic components of your new Marriage (see diagram) should be easily recognised and located (unless one or other of them is constantly 'Down the pub', 'Out with the boys', 'Out with the girls', 'Working late', etc.)

Getting to know how these major components operate will make tackling most regular maintenance, servicing and emergency repair tasks on your Marriage both simpler and less time-consuming.

GETTING INTO YOUR MARRIAGE: Only too easy. It's if you want to get <u>out</u> again that you may have problems (see Warning below).

1: Connect component (A) and component (B)

2: Disconnect old girlfriends/boyfriends

3: Jump into Marriage

4: Slam doors

Main components: (A) Husband, (B) Wife.

<u>WARNING</u>! Due to an unfortunate manufacturing fault which causes the doors of your Marriage to jam when slammed shut, you might experience difficulty getting in and out whenever it suits you (see 'Breakdown Procedures', page 24).

STARTING YOUR MARRIAGE: Note use of ignition key (Editor's note: We could, of course, have done a ruder version of this but didn't dare).

FUEL SYSTEM: Your new Marriage is fitted with an advanced fuel injection system – it requires regular injections of love and cash to keep it running smoothly. Fuel consumption varies greatly from one model to another and may also be seriously affected by bad driving habits (see 'Acceleration') or by overloading with passengers and non-standard optional equipment (see page 13).

CONTROLS

Take time to familiarize yourselves with the controls of your new Marriage before speeding off down life's great highway. They may just help you to avoid some of the worst bumps and potholes.

The most basic controls, and the most important for first-time Marriage owners to learn, include: Saying 'Yes', Saying 'No', and Putting Your Foot Down. Of course, there is absolutely no guarantee at all that these will work, but practice them anyway.

You should also note that your new Marriage is fitted with dual controls as standard. Try to agree on where you're going and how fast, to avoid conflicts over steering, acceleration, braking, etc.

STEERING: Due to basic design flaws, you may frequently feel that your Marriage is not going quite the way you'd like it to. It will greatly help if you can be sure that both you and your co-driver are steering in the same direction (see note on dual controls, above).

ACCELERATION: Harsh acceleration – trying to get to where you or your co-driver would eventually like to be (e.g. in a big house with three kids) too quickly – may result in excessive fuel consumption (see note on Fuel, below).

7

BRAKING: We regret that your Marriage is <u>not</u> equipped with all-round disc brakes as standard and may prove difficult to stop once you've started it (see 'Breakdown Procedures', page 24).

THROTTLE AND CHOKE: WARNING! Take care to avoid excessive use of <u>throttle</u> and <u>choke</u> , no matter how tempted you might be if your Marriage starts acting up. In breakdown situations, especially, this will only make matters worse.

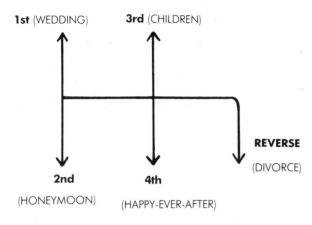

1st (WEDDING) **3rd** (CHILDREN)

REVERSE

(DIVORCE)

2nd **4th**

(HONEYMOON) (HAPPY-EVER-AFTER)

GEARS: Try to avoid slipping into <u>reverse</u> gear (see diagram above) instead of <u>4th</u> gear, by mistake. It's easily done; especially following excessive use of <u>3rd</u> gear.

COMFORT FEATURES

A range of special features have been designed into your new Marriage to make travelling in it a comfortable and enjoyable experience.

SEX-DRIVE: An invaluable feature of your Marriage, more or less essential for smooth running. Experimenting and twiddling with it should help to relieve the boredom of long journeys.

This is a standard feature on most models. If you find, on delivery of your new Marriage, that it has not been fitted or that any essential moving parts are missing (or do not move) this is a serious cause for complaint and may result in your Marriage being recalled to the factory.

SEX OVER-DRIVE: You should be so lucky!

WARNING! Excessive and indiscriminate use of sex-drive (see 'Bit On The Side' optional accessory, page 14) is likely to put additional strain on the main components of your Marriage, possibly resulting in serious breakdown.

SEXPENSION: (See also 'Sex-drive') The bouncy-bouncy bit of your Marriage. Helps to smooth out the bumps and potholes that you're bound to encounter along the way.

INTERIOR SPACE: Under normal driving conditions you should find that (depending on the model) your new Marriage provides ample leg-room and head-room. On long journeys, however, and especially if carrying small passengers (see page 13), things may get a bit cramped. It will help if you and your co-driver can give each other a little extra space from time to time. And in the event of a breakdown, you might find that you need to get out and stretch your legs for a while.

VENTILATION: We strongly recommend that you let some fresh air into your Marriage at regular intervals. Particularly if you need to clear the air during emergency breakdown procedures and repairs (see page 24), or if carrying especially pongy small passengers.

SAFETY FEATURES

BELTING-UP: For your own safety, we do <u>not</u> recommend that you constantly insist on your co-driver, and any small passengers in your Marriage, <u>belting up.</u> However, it <u>is</u> advisable for you to belt up yourself occasionally and give them a chance to have their say about where you are going in your Marriage.

<u>BACK-SEAT DRIVERS</u>: These <u>should</u> be told to belt up – unless they're coming out with constructive criticism about your driving, such as: "LOOK OUT!" or "OH, GOD! YOU'RE GOING TO CRASH!"

CHILDPROOF DEVICES: It is essential to make use of these if you don't want too many <u>little passengers</u> clambering about in your nice new Marriage and making revolting messes on the back seats. Your doctor or local family planning clinic will advise on suitable choices. Note that your Marriage is designed to carry a normal full load of 2 co-drivers and 2.5 small passengers. Try to avoid serious overloading, which may adversely affect performance and fuel consumption.

VISIBILITY: Under normal circumstances all-round visibility in your new Marriage should be excellent. But in bad driving conditions you may find that neither you nor your co-driver can see where your Marriage is going. Slow down and <u>take things easy</u> (see also 'Regular Maintenance and Servicing – Defrosting', page 17).

<u>WARNING</u>! Plastering 'Happy-Ever-After', 'Wedded-Bliss' and 'Made-In-Heaven' stickers all over the rear window and windscreen of your Marriage may obscure your view of the real world and cause a serious pile-up.

TOWING CAPACITY: <u>WARNING</u>! Your Marriage will <u>not</u> stand up to the strain of towing excessive loads.

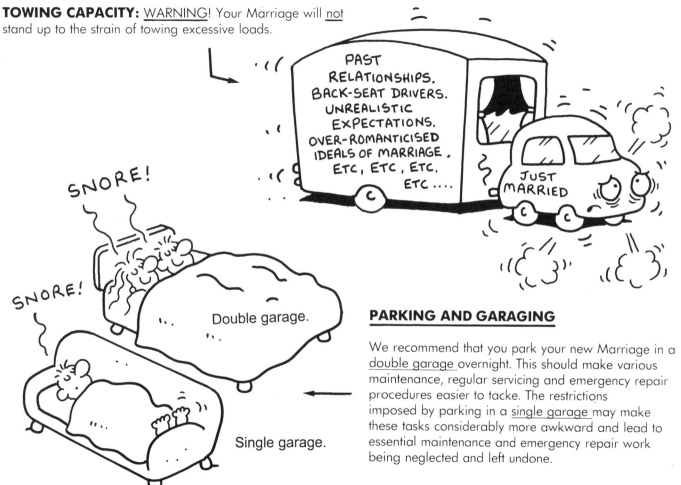

PAST RELATIONSHIPS. BACK-SEAT DRIVERS. UNREALISTIC EXPECTATIONS. OVER-ROMANTICISED IDEALS OF MARRIAGE. ETC, ETC, ETC, ETC....

JUST MARRIED

SNORE!

SNORE!

Double garage.

Single garage.

PARKING AND GARAGING

We recommend that you park your new Marriage in a <u>double garage</u> overnight. This should make various maintenance, regular servicing and emergency repair procedures easier to tacke. The restrictions imposed by parking in a <u>single garage</u> may make these tasks considerably more awkward and lead to essential maintenance and emergency repair work being neglected and left undone.

RECOMMENDED DRIVING POSITIONS

Talking   Not talking   Rowing   Making up

Sex-drive   ... ETC....

PERFORMANCE

Please do not expect your new Marriage to be a Ferrari or a Porsche. Performance may prove to be more on the lines of a Morris Minor. But then Morris Minors are reliable old bangers, virtually guaranteed to get you where you want to go. . . eventually.

UP-DATING TO A NEWER MODEL

This may seem tempting if you get fed up with your current Marriage. But it can prove expensive (see 'Breakdown Procedures', page 24) and you might well find that the new model displays the same faults and idiosyncracies that annoyed you in the old one. Then again, it could just be your driving that's at fault.

OPTIONAL FEATURES AND ACCESSORIES

Various non-standard features and accessories may
be fitted to your new Marriage at extra cost.
Please note that these can adversely affect
fuel consumption, so do think carefully before
attaching any or all of them.

PASSENGERS: Carrying <u>small passengers</u> in your
Marriage can add interest and entertainment value
to your journey. It also, however, greatly increases
fuel consumption (love/cash), results in noisier
operation, and may cause damage to the fabric
of your nice new Marriage. We strongly advise,
therefore, that you take care to <u>avoid overloading</u>.

<u>NOTE</u>: There is a nine-month waiting list for
delivery of <u>small passenger</u> components.

ROOF-RACK: This optional accessory allows you to load a vastly increased amount of <u>luggage</u> (carpets, three-piece suites, fridge-freezers, etc.) onto your new Marriage. Note that fitting costs can be high, and disconnection at a later date may prove difficult if house prices fall drastically. Can also have an extremely adverse effect on fuel consumption.

BIT-ON-THE-SIDE: Sticking bits on the side of your Marriage may look flashy but will <u>not</u> improve its performance. Indeed, adding this feature onto your Marriage may increase running costs and cause severe friction between the major components, leading to eventual breakdown. Should you feel that you need this optional accessory to help <u>get you out of a rut,</u> please note that it can equally well get your Marriage <u>onto a rocky road.</u>

Fitting is only too easy and may be performed by any DIY dick-head with the most basic of tools. However, disconnecting at a later date, should it cause running problems with your Marriage, can be a bit trickier. Note that careless fitting increases the risk of irreparable damage to your new Marriage. Skilfully connected, it should be unobstrusive and virtually invisible both from inside and outside the Marriage. Bung it on the roof or in the middle of the bonnet and you're just asking for trouble.

ROUTINE MAINTENANCE AND SERVICING

Regular maintenance and servicing is essential for the continued smooth-running of your New Marriage, and neglecting recommended routine procedures will greatly increase the chances of a serious breakdown. Trying to save time here is only likely to result in even more time and effort wasted on difficult and expensive emergency repair work later.

NOTE: We strongly recommended that at least once a year or every 10,000 miles you book your Marriage into an approved service-station/hotel for a thorough overhaul and M.O.T. (Marriage Operating Test). See Annual Service Record chart (page 20).

CHECKING MAIN COMPONENTS
1)   At regular intervals check that you still have both major components (Husband/Wife) and that one or other of these has not dropped out of your Marriage.
2)   Check for wear, especially if carrying small passengers in your Marriage. Worn-out components are a common problem and often a contributory factor in serious breakdowns.

REPLACEMENT PARTS: See 'Breakdown Procedures and Repairs' (page 24).

15

FUEL LEVELS: Your new Marriage runs best on a high-octane mixture of 4-star love and cash. If levels run low, your Marriage is likely to start backfiring and may eventually grind to a halt. Check levels frequently and don't expect your Marriage to run smoothly on a dry tank.

LUBRICATION: Regular lubrication reduces wear on major components and helps to prevent friction. It is _especially_ important if main components are under excessive strain (see 'Small Passengers', page 13). Recommended lubricants include: Multigrade TLC (Tender Loving Care) and Booze.

WARNING! Take care when topping up with Booze _not to overfill._ Constantly exceeding officially recommended levels can have a serious adverse effect on your Marriage's performance. Note: It is impossible to overfill when topping up your Marriage with TLC.

PRESSURES: Try to keep the pressures within your Marriage as _low_ as possible, and avoid putting too much pressure on your co-driver in disagreements about where you are going (see also 'Making Adjustments', in this section). Note that running pressure are likely to greatly increase if your Marriage is _overloaded_ or constanty driven at _high speed_ (see 'Small passengers', 'Roof Rack', 'Bit-On-The-Side' and 'Acceleration').

OVER-INFLATION WARNING! Try to avoid repeatedly over-inflating your problems, personal gripes and grumbles, blowing them up out of all proportion. This can adversely affect the performance of your new Marriage.

RUNNING TEMPERATURE: If your Marriage is not running smoothly or is heavily loaded (see 'Small Passengers', page 13), temperatures may rise sharply and without warning (note: this can also be caused by incorrect pressure settings; see above). Regular lubrication will help to reduce friction and prevent sudden rises in temperature. Note that in _frosty_ running conditions TLC (see 'Lubrication') acts as a dual-purpose lubricant and anti-freeze agent and will help to thaw things out a bit. Regular use of Sex-drive should also help to keep things warmed up and maintain optimum running temperatures.

BATTERY CHARGE: Check regularly and re-charge your batteries as often as possible at approved service-stations/hotels. Note that your batteries are likely to be especially low if constantly drained by small passengers (see page 13). Flat batteries may also contribute to poor sparking or failure to spark (see 'Sex-Drive').

SEX-DRIVE: Using the basic tool kit provided (and any specialist or kinky equipment you may find useful) check out this vital component whenever you and your co-driver feel like it – visually, manually, orally, and any other way you can think of without waking the neighbours or frightening domestic pets.

NOTE: Most Sex-drive operating checks may be performed without the aid of an inspection lamp; but it's more fun if you don't always insist on doing it with the lights off.

MAKING ADJUSTMENTS: You will probably find that you have to do a lot of this to keep your new Marriage running smoothly.

Please note that you and your co-driver will each have to make your own adjustments within the Marriage, so try to avoid using excessive force and do not over-tighten when 'putting the screws on' (see also 'Pressures').

CHECKING GAPS: Check occasionally to ensure that a wide gap has not developed between major components (Husband/Wife) due to wear-and-tear and excessive friction. Try to correct and adjust (see 'Lubrication', 'Sex-Drive' and 'Making Adjustments').

TIMING: You may often find that your timing could be better! This can only be improved by experience and trial-and-error, but do try to choose your moments carefully. See also 'Sex-Drive'.

POLLUTION: Your new Marriage should be comparatively non-polluting and environment-friendly. However, some <u>fuming</u> may be inevitable if your Marriage is not running smoothly, and especially during <u>breakdowns.</u> Regular maintenance and servicing will help to keep this to the minimum without the need to fit an expensive catalytic converter. <u>Very Small Passengers</u> may give off <u>considerable</u> air pollution in the form of noxious fumes, but there's not much you can do about this (see 'Your New Baby, An Owner's Manual', in the same series as this manual).

Note that excessively <u>noisy</u> operation (also inevitable in the event of breakdown or when carrying small passengers) may cause annoyance to neighbours.

CARE OF EXTERIOR FINISH: Giving your new Marriage an occasional wipe-over with a damp cloth will do no harm. But outward appearances are not all that important, and obsessional waxing, polishing, dusting and hoovering is <u>not</u> recommended (especially if time wasted on this is at the expense of more vital routine maintenance and servicing).

WARNING! Do please note, however, that obvious rust-patches, dents, bumps, bruises, black eyes, etc., indicate a serious lack of maintenance and servicing care and/or extremely careless driving habits which may lead to an irreparable breakdown or spectacular pile-up.

EASE OF MAINTENANCE: Having read this section, you may feel that keeping your new Marriage on the road and running smoothly involves a great deal of time-consuming effort and work. You betcha! It will, however, help if <u>both</u> of you work at it, <u>especially</u> when carrying <u>small passengers.</u>

SERVICE PERIOD	Honeymoon (running-in)	1st Anniversary (10,000 miles)	2nd Anniversary (20,000 miles)	3rd Anniversary (30,000 miles)
SERVICE STATION (HOTEL)				
♡ –LEVEL	Normal ☐ Low ☐	N ☐ L ☐	N ☐ L ☐	N ☐ L ☐
£–LEVEL	High ☐ Low ☐ Oh shit! ☐	H ☐ L ☐ O sht! ☐	H ☐ L ☐ O sht! ☐	H ☐ L ☐ O sht! ☐
SEX-DRIVE	High ☐ Low ☐ What? ☐	H ☐ L ☐ Wh? ☐	H ☐ L ☐ Wh? ☐	H ☐ L ☐ Wh? ☐
PASSENGERS (KIDS)	1 ☐ 2 ☐	1 ☐ 2 ☐ 3 ☐	1 ☐ 2 ☐ 3 ☐ 4 ☐	1 ☐ 2 ☐ 3 ☐ 4 ☐ 5 ☐
BATTERY CHARGE	High ☐ Low ☐ Flat ☐	H ☐ L ☐ F ☐	H ☐ L ☐ F ☐	H ☐ L ☐ F ☐
M.O.T. (MARRIAGE OPERATING TEST)	Pass/Fail	Pass/Fail	Pass/Fail	Pass/Fail

FAULT DIAGNOSIS

Finding fault with your Marriage is easy. The difficult part is doing something about it (see 'Routine Maintenance and Servicing', and 'Breakdown Procedures and Emergency Repairs'). But you can't fix what you don't know needs fixing, so the following trouble-shooting chart and check-list are designed to help pin-point general problem areas and specific faults before they develop into a serious breakdown situation.

CHECK-LIST OF MAJOR FAULTS

MARRIAGE WILL NOT START: Check you have both major components (Husband/Wife). Check fuel levels (♥ and £). Check Sex-drive (see page 9).

MARRIAGE STARTS, BUT MISFIRES AND GRINDS TO A HALT:
Check you still have both major components. Check fuel levels. Check lubricant levels (page 17). Check for a carelessly-fitted Bit On The Side optional add-on accessory (page 14) interfering with normal running and performance.

MARRIAGE GOING IN WRONG DIRECTION
Slow down and consult co-driver. Check map-reading. Check which of you is trying to steer, and whether you're both steering in the same direction (note that Marriage is fitted with dual controls, see page 7). Check whether either of you is map-reading or steering.

21

NOISY RUNNING: This is <u>perfectly normal,</u> expecially when carrying <u>small passengers</u> (page 13) in your Marriage. However, excessive noise (shouting, yelling, screaming, etc) <u>other</u> than from Small Passengers may indicate impending breakdown and a need for emergency repairs.

<u>Silent</u> running: <u>Not</u> normal. Check you still have both major components (Husband/Wife) and Small Passengers (if appropriate). If you do, check whether you're still talking.

<u>Knocking</u> noises: If your co-driver is constantly 'knocking' you, putting you down, and criticising your driving, this also warrants urgent attention (if all else fails, a sharp tap with a large adjustable spanner may do the trick; otherwise, see 'Breakdown Procedures', page 24).

<u>Rumbling</u> noises: Should you notice annoying rumblings of discontent from within your Marriage, the best way to diagnose the exact problem is to slow down and <u>listen carefully.</u>

EXCESSIVE FUEL CONSUMPTION: Marriage may be overloaded. Check for <u>Small Passengers</u> (page 13) and count them (see also 'Childproof Devices', page 10). Check <u>Roof Rack</u> (page 14). Check for <u>Bit On The Side.</u> Try to avoid <u>harsh acceleration</u> (see page 7).

FARP!

FINDING-FAULT CHART

Tick your co-driver's (Marriage partner's) faults on the following chart as you discover them, then leave where he/she is bound to accidentally find it. Mark any requiring especially urgent attention with a '!'

MY MARRIAGE PARTNER'S MOST GLARING AND BLATANT FAULTS ARE:

Snores like a walrus		Farts in bed		Falls asleep straight after nookies	
Eats like a pig		Squeezes spots at breakfast table		Falls asleep during nookies	
Has smelly feet/armpits		Wants five children		Drinks too much	
Has chronic dandruff		Does not want five children		Nags me for drinking too much	
Doesn't talk		Is interfering/nosey		Won't do fair share of housework	
Doesn't listen		Is not interested in what I do		Won't help look after kids	
Doesn't think		Is overbearing and bossy		God, how did I ever get stuck with this gross nurd?	
Is a lazy sod		Is a wimp and a doormat			
Is a boring old fart		Constantly flirts with other men/ women/domestic pets/inanimate objects		Other annoying mannerisms, traits and disgusting personal habits (please specify, giving lurid details)	
Is fat/spotty					
Is as thick as a brick		Spends too much on himself/herself			
Picks nose		Doesn't spend enough on me			

BREAKDOWN PROCEDURES AND EMERGENCY REPAIRS

Your new Marriage is less likely to develop serious faults requiring extensive and costly repairs if recommended maintenance and servicing procedures are carried out regulary and competently. However, you should always be prepared for an unexpected breakdown due to the normal wear-and-tear of daily running and/or failure to spot the warning signs.

WARNING LIGHTS: These should start to flash if any or all of the following problems start to develop (see previous section for further details):

- ♥ fuel-gauge registers empty
- TLC reservoir dry
- Sex-drive inoperative (or only operating with Bit-On-The-Side optional accessory fitted to Marriage)
- Overheating (temperatures rising sharply)
- Excessively noisy running (especially constant screams of "STOP! I WANT TO GET OUT!!")

WHAT TO DO: If your Marriage has not completely ground to a halt, drive <u>very slowly</u> to a service-station/hotel for a complete overhaul and/or book into an approved <u>Marriage Guidance Workshop</u> for specialist fault-diagnosis.

If your Marriage stops and will not start again, the following procedures should be adopted as quickly as possible:

(A) Put out HAZARD WARNING SIGNS so that other Marriage owners can <u>steer clear</u> of you if they don't want to get tangled up in your wreckage (especially important if they're having trouble controlling their own Marriages and the last thing they need is to get involved in a multiple pile-up).

Procedure for putting out HAZARD WARNING SIGNS: Whinge, whine, grumble, nag, sulk, squabble, yell, scream, fight, complain constantly to friends, relatives and work colleagues, blame everyone but yourself, get pissed, get abusive, get morose, get boring, get paranoid, get lawyers (not necessarily in this order).

(B) Try to ATTRACT ATTENTION and GET HELP. Much the same procedure as for putting out Hazard Warning Signs (see above) and unfortunately may tend to have the same effect. So don't be surprised if you don't get too many other Marriage owners stopping to lend a hand. Alternatively, contact your nearest approved Marriage Guidance Workshop for a tow.

Note: If broken down and unable to get going again, you may feel like taking the opportunity to get out of your Marriage and stretch your legs for a while. If so, try to arrange to meet up with your co-driver later at the Marriage Guidance Workshop, to assess the damage and consult over repairs/scrapping.

EMERGENCY REPAIRS

WARNING! OVERHEATING PROBLEMS: If temperatures have risen sharply prior to breakdown, take care to allow time for things to cool down a little before attempting any emergency repairs, otherwise you may risk getting your fingers burned.

GETTING YOU GOING AGAIN: In an emergency, try the following basic procedure (but note that more extensive repairs and thorough servicing may be needed later):
1) TALK
2) LISTEN
3) DO SOMETHING

EMERGENCY REPAIR KIT: We strongly advise that you try to ensure you have at least a basic selection of these useful tools with you at all times. Most will come in equally handy during routine maintenance and servicing:

Tolerance, patience, understanding, forgiveness, assertiveness, sense of humour, supportive friends and relatives, flowers, lots of TLC (see 'Lubrication', page 17), a willing ear, a shoulder to cry on, a bloody miracle.

USE of the above repair kit should be self-explanatory. If you're not familiar with even the most basic tools and how to use them, call an expert mechanic immediately (see 'Marriage Guidance Workshops' earlier in this section). Even if you are a keen DIY enthusiast, we still strongly urge that you obtain some expert fault-diagnosis and advice since a bodged repair job may only result in a more serious breakdown later on.

NOTE: You will need adequate elbow-room when working on repairs to your Marriage. Try to give one another plenty of SPACE.

SPARE PARTS: Due to manufacturing and supply problems, you may find that brand new replacements for old major components (Husband/Wife) in <u>perfect</u> working order might not be as readily available as you'd expect. You may end up making do with a replacement component in <u>less than perfect</u> condition or which displays much the same annoying faults as the old one.

For these reasons, we strongly urge that you try to make original components last as long as possible. Note that correct maintenance and servicing will greatly extend the useful working life of all parts of your new Marriage. In the event of a serious breakdown, it is always worth investigating whether it's possible to get the old components reconditioned at a Marriage Guidance Workshop.

CHANGING A MARRIAGE PARTNER:

1. Jack-up bed
2. Remove old partner
3. Fit new partner and lower bed

28

SCRAPPING/WRITING-OFF YOUR MARRIAGE:

We recommend that you check with an experienced Marriage Guidance mechanic that your Marriage is a complete write-off before taking it to a scrap-merchant/lawyer for breaking.

NOTE: Do not expect a scrap-merchant/lawyer to pay you for the scrap value of your old Marriage. You're more likely to end up paying through the nose for them to take it away (especially if towing charges have to be added to the bill, for dragging it at great length through the divorce courts).

YOUR NEW MARRIAGE'S TECHNICAL SPECIFICATIONS

FUEL TYPES AND AVERAGE CONSUMPTION:
4-star ♡ and £: Consumption variable, depending on
driving technique and load (see Recommeded Max. Load)

RECOMMENDED LUBRICANTS (WITH CAPACITIES):
Multigrade TLC (Capacity; bottomless)
Booze (Capacity limited; take care not to
        exceed officially-recommended levels)

RECOMMENDED MAXIMUM LOAD:
Driver, 2; Small Passengers, 2.5; Backseat Drivers, 0

CHANCES OF BREAKDOWN IN FIRST 10 YEARS:
Under normal driving conditions: 40% (official)
After addition of Small Passengers: 40%–100% (depending on number)
After addition of Bit-On-The-Side optional accessory; 99%–100%

NORMAL ROAD-LIFE EXPECTANCY:
See 'Chances Of Breakdown In First 10 Years'

POLLUTION CONTROLS:
None fitted as standard. Some fuming and excessive
noise is normal and only to be expected (especially
if carrying Small Passengers).
Note: Your new Marriage should not pump harmful lead
into the air (unless one or other of the co-drivers
gets his or her hands on a gun during a serious
breakdown situation.)

YOUR NEW BABY

AN OWNER'S MANUAL

MODEL 1001A-GIRL
MODEL 1001B-BOY

Also available in this series is **YOUR NEW BABY, An Owner's Manual,** an invaluable and hugely popular in-depth guide to operating, maintaining and servicing one of the most important features of your new Marriage, guaranteed to ensure many years of trouble-free operation.

"I don't know what I would have done without your wonderful New Baby manual – I had no idea how to work my new Baby properly and thought it might be some kind of novel food-blender until I read your marvellous hand-book." (unsolicited letter from a reader, Mr. A.N. Idiot of Milton Keynes).

OTHER BOOKS BY MARTIN BAXENDALE:

'THE SNOWDROP GARDEN' - Martin's first novel is a wickedly funny and heart-warming tale of love, misunderstandings and a last-ditch attempt to save one of England's most beautiful woodland snowdrop gardens from the builders' bulldozers. A really great, laugh-out-loud read.

'WHEN WILL MY BABY BRAIN FALL OUT?' - Martin's first children's book. Seven-year-old Millie struggles with her maths homework but then she gets hold of the idea that things will be better when her 'baby brain' falls out, just like a baby tooth, and her cleverer big-girl brain grows in its place. Should Mum and Dad put her straight or play along? A very funny yet charming story that will have children laughing out loud.

And some of Martin's best-selling cartoon gift-books:

'Your New Baby, An Owner's Manual' (over 500,000 copies sold).
'How To Be A Baby, An Instruction Manual For Newborns'
'Your Marriage, An Owner's Manual'
'How To Be Married, An Instruction Manual For Newlyweds'
'Life After 40, A Survival Guide For Women'
'Life After 40, A Survival Guide For Men'
'Life After 50, A Survival Guide For Women'
'Life After 50, A Survival Guide For Men'
'How To Stay Awake During Sex (and other handy hints on coping with old age)'
'Martin Baxendale's Better Sex Guide'
'The Relationship Survival Guide'
'A Very Rude Book About Willies'
'The Cat Owner's Survival Guide'
'The Dog Owner's Survival Guide'
'Your Man, An Owner's Manual'
'Calm Down!! The Stress Survival Guide'
'Your Pregnancy, A Survival Guide'
'Women Are Wonderful, Men Are A Mess'

These and other books by Martin Baxendale can be ordered from www.amazon.co.uk (search for Martin Baxendale, or search by title, in 'books') and from other online bookstores or any High Street bookshop.